Cantata for Jimmy

RASHIDAH ISMAILI

Africa World Press, Inc.

P.O. Box 1892
Trenton, NJ 08607

P.O. Box 48
Asmara, ERITREA

Africa World Press, Inc.

P.O. Box 1892   P.O. Box 48
Trenton, NJ 08607   Asmara, ERITREA

Book & Cover Design: Roger Dormann
Cover Art: With the permission of Tafa

Library of Congress Cataloging-in-Publication Data

Ismaili, Rashidah.
 Cantata for Jimmy / Rashidah Ismaili.
  p. cm.
 ISBN 1-59221-158-5 (cloth) — ISBN 1-59221-159-3 (pbk.)
 I. Title.

PS3559.S56C36 2003
821'.914—dc22

2003022150

Table of Contents

A, My Name Is 4
Jimmy's Song 5
Un-named 6
Grief and Pain, 1st Person Singular 7
Inception, 2nd Person Singular 8
Jimmy Sings 9
Historiography 10
Harlem Nuances 12
Cinema Verite 13
Symptoms 16
There Was a Dream 18
Flare Up 19
Roach 22
Early Days 24
Contagion 26
Medication 29
Phantom 30
A Long Road 32
Roach-2 32
Traveling 34
Get on Board 36
And I Came Crying 38
Ritual 40
Walk Together Children 45
Bridges 47
Paris 50
Return 52
La Neige 54
The End 56

A, My Name Is

Three fathers ago
earth was sure
underfoot rocks
fetid soil, scorpions
and snakes were
familiar to see,
to touch.

Eyes upon a sea
that watered seeds
opened hundreds
of years later.

Pods breaking open
to let in light
out pours life.
Eyes of a seer
lips of a lover
words spill
overflowing
liquor.

In this age of truth
where magic is suspect,
who will kiss a prince
imprisoned inside a frog?

Jimmy's Song

O-or-ri-ri Orisha.
Kh-kh-kh-ki
Kini? Kini se nko?
Kini? Iya! Iya!
Pele, pele omode!
Baba! Baba!
Ma! Mami!

Woooooooooeee!

"I told Jesus
be alright if He..."
"Oruko me amaje
Babatunde. Ayi!
Iya! Iya! Ba, Babu.
Bu Bubba!

"I told Jesus,
be alright
if He changed my name.
If He changed my name"

Oruko me amaje bubba.
Me dey call Bubba. But
in the oddeh place, me
dey call Babatunde.

Ayi! Ayi! Mami! Iya!

"A long way from home."

Un-named

Calcified moments
a past I dare re-claim.
and in these new words
signed in a new name.
I the witness,
life's mirror, reflect.
Reflect.
Will answer when called.

But you know.
It's okay.
Cause,
"I told Jesus
be alright
if He changed my name.
Changed my name
Changed my name."

Grief and Pain
1st Person Singular

From warmth and darkness
from inside to outside
I breathe, ahhhhhh.
Inflating a new pair of lungs.

I was an unknown.
Now, she knows me.
But one name cannot,
dare not be spoken.

She has a mouth
but will not tell me.
So, I am he
who has a ?
for surname.

Ah well,
that's alright.
Everyone has a right
to privacy,
to secrets. Anyway,
to know is to blame.

So I invent a time
and add an X.

"A, my name is…."

Inception

Uu-u-oo-ah
Wa-wa-wa,
Ma-mi, Ma-mi
Da-da, Da-da.
Smack! Smack! Shhh!

It is long and hard.
The arduous route
from inside a sac
cushioned
in a sea
whose currents
expel fish
and swimmer
onto a waiting bed
or sandy shore.

Rude and harsh
lights
air invades
skin and lungs
trying to expand
to rise to the
occasion.

Jimmy Sings

In song sounds travel.
Swirls of dust made
by fleeing feet, moving.
Moving but not knowing,
not caring. Just going.

There is a hum brought
from across the seas,
locked up in a ship.
It is washed and stored
deep inside slave huts.

An unidentified melody persists.
Stubborn arms cling to a spot

I kiss the air in which butterflies
glide and prayers wing their way
to open space.

Sweat and skin mix
beating rhythms
dancers caught
in a maelstrom,
swim in frenzy where
a memory box is hid.
There ancestral voices
speak in unknown tongues.

Listen. They are calling.
"Kai, kai fi!" And "Brah,
brah Mami." And "Omode,
Babatunde."

Jimmy sings, "But the wicked
carried me away, captivity
requires from me a song.
How can I sing in a strange land?"

Historiography

Grains of sand rasping
underfoot receding, wet;
carving a footprint
to be washed away
without a trace.

Egotistic needs
to make permanent;
a mark, a sign,
that life and limbs
combined on this spot
gutted out of feces
and waste of creatures
with no voice

whose lives go un-noticed
from eon to eon.
Yet still water is in the seas
and progeny swim.
My feet sink deep beneath
hot sand to feel cool grains
dissolve under my soles.

And this is my claim to earth.
This small space holding me
upright with sun and sky
on my head. Sand ants at foot.
These are elements of force
keeping humanity
walking on two feet.

And so, sky above earth
below me in the middle,
stretched between opposites
who must needs exists
against tide and time.
Their boats heave and dip,

rock and creak.
Then they are thrust
out onto the sea.
Clutching at straws,
weaving a life-line
from hairs of heads.

High above turbulent seas
birds dare the air with song
and at each note a cloud recedes
timbre vibrates against crash
of thunder and gulls screech
over oceans roar.
They, the swimmers, pull
up to shore and breath rasps
in their chest and sea foam
bubbles from mouths ajar.

On sand, disturbed ants curious,
angrily seek to know dislocated
ripples and clogged holes.
They rush.
They bite.
They bury their stinger
inside crevices of old sores.
Holes gaping, smarting
from salt water.
Ahh, torture. Ahh revenge.
This is unkindness.

Harlem Nuances

She is a descriptive term
sitting on stoops
too tired to walk.
A narration squeezed
inside skin stretched
to contain bulges
overweight has caused.

Her dreams have turned
to sugar and gangrene
rots her legs but her eyes
are sharp and strong.

Experience has shaded
her youthful poetry.
Time waits on corners
watered by bloods and dogs.

Sometimes at night
she thinks she hears
the sounds history
has recorded.

Her lights are out.
The current is dead.
Candles have ways
with forms.

The Story is locked
in beads and braids,
smells of peach snuff
and sweet sweat.

She will rise one day
on new legs with fresh skin.
Then dance down to the river
waving her young ones home.

Cinema Verite

Silence and secrets are waiting
still, in the night. Wanting.
Sorrow hidden.
The sun sleeps till tomorrow.
Poverty is respectful at night.
But oh, come sundown
the faithful are always rewarded.
They do not question tranquility
floating on salty waves that
kiss empty market stalls.

The boats have gone.
Streets are quiet.
Avenues are freed
of people. But,
at night the heart,
still wanting, slows to rest.

Windows refuse to budge.
Time-worn-hemp is frayed.
Wood work, dirt grounded.
They cannot be cleaned.
The windows cannot be cleaned
within the confines of tired air.

The workers laugh and chat
Men and machine speak
one to the other.
All eyes are focused on him.

He speaks, the Boss.
His mouth begins to move.
Those who doubted he was there
tucked away behind the second door,
at the end of the corridors.
See. the words fall from his lips.
Changes are coming down the way.

New methods and machines
for those who can, the tide
will find them ready to drift
downstream. But for those
who cannot swim, it will be
rough on them.
Windows now are open.
You can see the street below.
Fewer machines but wider aisles
make life pleasant for some.
Dust no longer gathers in corners.
Suction sees to that.
Old men with handkerchiefs
over their mouths and throats
have suddenly disappeared.

There is no rest for workers.
Their time is not their own.
Machines or masters either one.
They call in angry tones
of arrogance and privy.

Days are long with short divides.
Bones ache inside where NO's
are stored and rebellion foments.
Still, backsides sway, arms loose
and, heads are high.
Homeward bound are they.
Bodies fitted into bargains
bringing extra work to some.

There is neither rest nor air
during cold or heated days.
Window washers come
on Mondays. The Boss
is in at ten.
He leaves early
and calls on Wednesdays
before the bookkeepers leaves.

The books are balanced
and workers are fewer.
Wages are higher
but the crew is shortened.
Each week it seems
a new face replaces age.

The windows are cleaned regularly.
Offices have been enlarged.
There are two ladies room now
with a lounge and coffee machine.
Each week a new dress.
Every month new pants.
Food is dearer.
Someone is on a diet.

Television replaces dialogue.
There is no one to talk.
Machines cannot love.
They cannot kiss away
emptiness that clean windows
expose. Corners without dust
no longer hide the shadow
of a dream.

Symptoms

Each day dawns with less force.
Cries of hunger dulled by lack
of response of rains
simpers in silence
with no expectation.

Waiting is learned early.
Clocks wind down.
Minutes eclipse hours.
At some moment
a thing is thrust inside another.
Into a young mouth waiting

systemic pull-pull brings milk
or pap into a flaccid stomach.
Belches and dried dribble are licked
by friendly creatures who
sit around a neglected crib.

This is a child who learns early
neither cries nor holds
outstretched arms
to an approaching face. A hand
extends with a dry diaper.

Shifting laps in a safe house,
an infantile body grows.
So too grows the frequency
of blows and missed meals,
torn shirts.

Caretakers become radio.
A worn bible, a staple of life.
Turned over to a god
who watches mysterious,
imperious; white and bloody
hangs above a door

leading to a kitchen.
One passes under daily
an icon of white
to reach a fridge,
then back to a sitting room
with sofa, sugar-starch doilies
poised on dark wood tabletops.
Encircling plastic flowers
forever in high bloom.
They cannot die.
They have not lived.

Untutored young eyes
seeking to map out
terrain friendly to feet
to locate a stationary
from mobile path.

Love hardly kisses him goodnight.
Scarcely licks sleep from his eyes
when the sun slips in and blinds him.
But comes, hands without softness
takes a cold rag, washes his soft
bed-warm-face and goes off,
without so much as a
"By your leave."

There Was a Dream

Distilled in blue transparency
his dreams, rare old bottles,
antiseptic and sterile;
untouched and untried,
the cases upon cases
heaped beneath dustbins.

Piled on top of pages and pages
penmanship a practiced art,
a calligraphic ornamentation,
a would-be-barrister.

He would have been a lawyer
had his hair behaved;
flowed to his shoulders.
He could have sat law
and read the fine print
of all the whys and wherefores
punctuating his briefs
with "Hu-rumphs" and "Uh-ruhs."

He would have looked fine
in his flowing black robes.
His wig white puffs
encasing his black face.

But death and dire circumstances
shelved his dreams and pushed
his hopes further and further
in a dusty corner.

He might have been a lawyer
instead of just someone's father
who comes home dead tired
and snores loudly in an unfriendly night.

Flare Up

She moved strangely
across a small floor.
He watched her nearing.
There was a familiar smile
caught in the corner
of her wide mouth.
He thought he'd seen her before.
Sometime ago when he was younger.

She moved, floated by.
Her hand brushed his cheek.
His face felt warm.
His heart beat fast.
Images raced in his head
looking for a name

to place the face.
He watched. She ate.
He stalked. She paced
up and down the hall
of his grandmother's flat.

She scratched her head often.
Her hands seemed to reach
for something in her bag.
They stopped mid-way, empty.
She trembled each time
the phone rang, knock at the door.

Why? No one answered his stare.
He never offered questions.
His words formed inside
a private space where
he talked to himself
in his own language.
His grandmother and aunts
spent evening, all nights

praying for her lost soul.
"Come ye dis-con-so-late.
Where-ere-ere ye lang-anguish.
Come to the Mercy Seat."

And a chorused, "Yes Lord!
Hal-lay-loo-ya Jee-ssus!"
The woman on the couch
stared ahead with blank eyes.

Roach had not learned to read
this type of page. So he sat
as the words fell on both.
"...words of my mouth
and the medi-ta-tion of my heart."
All the voices blended
into shimmering sounds.

The room was lit with music
holding them ransomed
to the moment. She got up
and let her body move
out of her dress. No! No!
What was it she wore?
Ah well, no matter.

He would come back to it later.
Give it his name, his word.
In the meantime, this female form
danced before the host in her
bare blackness. Lighted by
blinking neon: "Eat well,
24 hours." Then he felt
his small body lifted.

He found himself on a soft mat.
For the first time, a human hand
loved him. Loved him.
Kissed his fleshy lips.
The Lord is love.

He, Roach awakened
to find his um, 'thing'
was staring, uh, standing
above him.

A haze halved her face. A laugh
played on her lips. She opened
her mouth to let a sound, "Hee-hee."
She held him to her breast
and he was suckled.
Yet still his um, 'thing'
stuck up awkward between them.
A cloud engulfed them.
Roach entered a dark tunnel.
At each turn he felt déjà vu.
"I've been here before."
Somewhere along the way
he stumbled, lost his 'thing.'

But then, the sunset.
The moon arrived, rose, fell.
Then darkness. "Harlot!
Harlot!" Violence of sound.
Murder in a voice with words
banging against his head.

Scarcely had he time
to translate People
into his language
before he felt cold.
Ice poured down on him.

The haze vanished
and silence of his voice
was replace by shrill
and accusations.
All that was important
was Love and It walked away.
The long black female body
came no more.

Roach

"Roach," that is what everyone called him.
Him! No, he didn't eat them. Just said so.
Just to make them leave him alone.
Not to try to silence words in his head.
To steal, change his self-language.

He spoke Roach, Cat, and some Dog.
They taught him their tongues when
he was empty of his sound. Before
Grandmother's songs he sang Pigeon
in early awakening morning.

He grew big to spite gifts of welfare-salted butter,
yellow coloured cheeses and white everything;
white rice, white flour, white sugar, white fat.
Only peanut butter with oil on top was brown.

When he walked the streets he felt the space
People put between him and them. Glad!
He was glad that this was what he could do.
His lessons taught by a past where
he was assaulted by half-formed shapes.

Daily non-recognition of him, his mother,
father, grandmother and, all the others
who looked like him and those who lived
all around. him. And from them he knew,
knew that death was not what he saw nightly
on a small black and white TV with a hanger
for an antennae. That dead men lost their hats.
Blood was not red dye. Flesh infected
would pus and run if squeezed.
He knew all of this.

When he walked he looked ahead
and let sounds fall on his ears.
He had the power of Roach
to close his holes and then
'They' could not enter him
Not there in that space where
he stored in a secret place
pictures, words and scraps
of cloth from discarded clothes.
So he walked and walked lifting, dropping
his shield if and when he pleased.
His lips parted in a smile.
Only he held the key to it.
The truth, his truth he created
out of the bits of coloured strips
of flotsam under foot.

Early Days

It was time.
He listened
when THEY
moved
THEIR lips
to say things.
They did not know
he had learned to 'hear'
these things that fell
from the two pieces
of flesh at the bottom
of THEIR FACE.

So, it was time he went to school.
Well, he might, might go.
Squash, his brother told him
about that place. He and Squash
always spoke Roach together.
Squash lived with his family
behind a big thing where
THEY put food.
Squash had never been inside one
but, he told him there was enough
to feed the entire block. Cat, Dog,
Rat and even Pigeon.

Squash said his cousin
had gone inside once
with a friend who knew
how to get in and out.
But his cousin did not know
to lower his body heat.
One of THEM opened the door
and he escaped—barely missing
a big shadow that made a clash
on the floor. THEY called this
a foot. Anyway, Squash and the rest

thought it a good idea for him to go
to learn THEIR talk. After all,
he is a PEOPLE. He should say PEOPLE.
So he let his grandmother move
her slit flesh and 'heard' her sounds
because he opened his holes/ears.
That night all his friends, families
came to him when grandmother
went to church leaving him asleep.
They partied! Dog and Cat danced.
Rat got down with Hamster behind
Grandfather's chair. They all saw them.
Mama Squoosh kissed him.
She said she would send Junior
to keep him company.

So Roach put his head
on a bleach-worn pillow-case
that testified to his grandmother's code
of goodness. Soon he slept.
Mama Squoosh, Cat, Rat and Squash
licked his face and lulled him to sleep.

Contagion

Three flat concrete steps toward
marbled halls where fluorescent
lights up dirt ground black
speckled, waxed and hardened.

A world contained by hardwood chairs
forcing a backside to sit upright
or slump, half-hidden behind
a thing called desk, upon which
one writes names, addresses
and other vital information.

There is a blackboard, two windows.
At the back pegs for coats, hats.
It is a place defined by rows of desks
designs etched deep in wood,
names, dates and heart shapes.

A People came in and opened its slits.
Roach heard its sounds, translated
some of it, left the rest. Became bored,
opened his brown lunch and saw Junior.
"Ugh!" a baby People pointed with
a rounded mouth.

A big People came near,
moving lips, hands and words.
His bag snatched plopped
into a gray can with paper.
A 'sssister,' sounded death
in Roach. "Junior!"

His grandmother had one too.
It plopped Squoosh's uncle,
brothers and sisters.
Roach smiled when he saw Junior
raise his hand under the can.
Up his leg, into his pocket
Roach felt his little friend.

Roach, careful lest someone hear
he spoke to Junior and quieted his heart.
The People all around moved far.
Their nose pointed to the ceiling
and words hid behind hands.
Roach did not mind the distance
enjoyed the space between
friends and foes.

That night, in his room, books
and pencil lay on his bed.
His sound-maker hurt.
He could not swallow.
When asked he could not tell.
Grandmother spoke People
when the telephone rang.

The Big People, called Teacher
said that he was dirty and that
bugs came with his lunch.
Grandmother made a Sunday.
The Book was opened.
She took his hand.
They knelt beside a chair.
She called "Jee-sus"
and "Lord You know.
Take this little one
lead him along."

Roach went back to his room.
His friends waited in a secret space.
He lay in the dark and remembered
sun shining on him, his street.
All night he saw moonbeams
promising the magic of People
spread out on a white page
with words in black. Black
like him they waited for his lips
to break the spell and say
the letters waiting for him
to give them life.

Medication

Roach was caught between
Grandmother, her lap and belt.
She met him in Sunday,
where People sounded Church.
Grandfather was Saturday and hair.
He was "glug-glug" and "nnkn" sleep.

As Roach sounded People
he stopped making Human.
There was no more rain.
He was dry. His flesh hardened.
His holes were Dog.
He opened one, closed the other.
The last sound he heard
was Grandfather, water, washing.

Roach heard Cat, Dog, and Rat
as they slept. He dreamed
he was a baby slipping
from a leftover plate,
half empty, sliding onto a bed.
His um 'thing' hardened
remembering a tunnel
and a People who had come
warmed his unclothed body
and disappeared.

"Yes Jee-sus loves me.
Yes Jee-sus loves me."

Phantom

A shadow moves across the wall.
Scrape-scrape, the flip-flops
scratch against resistant
lino-waxed sheen petrified.

She is familiar.
This big-belly woman
stirring a pot, is singing
"Yes, Jee-sus loves me."

There is a phantom
ghosting the kitchen.
She comes and goes
at nine-month intervals.

Waiting for disappearance-
reappearance, to catch
a glimpse of brown
squirms bundled
against drafts, all wait.

The red-eye monster
hiding in the cupboard,
under a table and chairs waits.

The silence broken by
"Screech-screech"
announces, the phantoms
are doing 'It.' Fear!
Soon she will leave
taking with her
smells of chicken
and peppered gravy.

Ah, the scent of return,
sour milk and mustard.
Ah, the sound of forays
quiet at midnight.
Ah, Christmas-time odors,
that means dull white walls
and maybe a tree.
Stale Dixie Peach, olive oil
mixed with roses and cloves
cloak her hair and body.
Caught in closeness
of lips to cheek, breathes
warm. A light touch is all.
You cannot hold too tight
a ghost. It will vanish.
And Roach hates being alone.

A Long Road
Roach-2

I've walked roads that ended
in opened fields, where dogs
ran wild and chased me,
where haunted houses
and trees danced
without breezes.

I've stopped to rest
on broken stumps.
Bathed in snake-water,
watched tadpoles hatch,
slapped mosquito songs.
I have crushed bloodsuckers
between my fingers.

Yet all the time,
a rolling ball of yarn
unravels in a puss' paw.
Helpless, hurled into space,
a place set aside at an hour
appointed. I've kept my date
with my kith and kin; lover and foe.

In days since then I have cried
and laughed waiting for the end
where the road curves. But oh,
the road's been hard and long.

Sometimes I have yearned
for the feel of water,
longed to rest. Hungered
for a companion
a hand to hold,
a shoulder to keep me together.
These were the times
when I was given stone for bread.

But, in moments, a smile
from a passing child
sounds of laughter,
have come to rest on my ears,
I have rejoiced.
The sun will set,
the moon will rise
and the road will go on
winding. And I shall
go on and on.

Traveling
Frog Eyes

It is with lover-soft feet
I tread closer. Trembling,
I come singing. "Lord, Lord,
here I am." Singing
in a faint voice, "God,
oh God, how come I here?"
Searching for answers
in whispering palms,
on blossoms of cotton boughs.
In work-beckoning lengths
of cane rows, I cry out.

Send the birds to the sky.
Send the fish to the sea.
Bring their secrets to ease
our worried souls.

With soft singing, daring
stilled air space, to mix
a tune in spiced nights
where soft winds bring
sounds of salty sea;
wind sprinkles sand
on jagged cliffs
and exposes the sky.

Tell the moon and stars
who watch from so far
at safe distance, how
tired feet feel from
sand pebbles and heavy work.
How eyes lose their sight
for yellow and orange butterflies;
red-flowered trees, when the sun
blends them in cotton fields.
How in dim-dust factories
vision fades.

Send the birds to the sky.
Send the fish to the sea.
Bring their secrets
to soothe empty arms
in tear-filled rooms
where joy seldom visits.

Baby-just-born-feet,
aged and elusive feet,
faltering, fleeing;
exchanging open fields
for box cars and cement,
for subways, buses
and doilies laden
with cotton dresses.

Processed hair covered
under black scarves,
locks and braids;
platforms, shoes
sandals and shades
all progressing
from one street to the next.
There, where sad songs
are sung apart-ment.

Send the birds to the sky.
Send the fish to the sea.
Bring their secrets to me.
Bring me a freedom song.

Jubilation! Jubilation!

Get on Board
Roach-3

It sounds Saturday.
People move, dance
when they talk People.

It is after Pigeon
has gone to look
for food for two.

Beyond my window/eyes
Grandfather takes me
to his hair place where
People is spoken fast

sliding off lips, cracked,
laughing in their bellies.
Where feet step on
two-weeks growth
pass from a fortnight.
Splashes smells that
hurt my win—eyes tear.

It sounds Saturday
when we come home
and Grandmother fires
Bee's wax. Speaks them
pies, cakes.

My snout/nose laughs.
My stomach sounds/Dog
when he comes in my room
along with the sun.
It is Saturday and Grandfather
goes off with gabardine.
Makes tingles in his pockets.
Rubs his feet against
suited pant legs.

Cat-without fur.
Grandmother washes floors.
She raises linos looking
but Mama Squoosh and family
have moved to a new location.
I told them to hide
under Grandmother's
Sunday/ Bible.
Under the cloth
they would be safe
from the ssister
that zapped Junior's uncle
and cousin only last week.

It smells Saturday in my room.
Fresh sheets and clothes
ironed, waiting for the sun
and Grandmother
to come fetch me.

My eyes are heavy.
I get up to make Sunday.

"Now I lay me down to sleep."

And I Came Crying

Holy is his name.
(What is in a name?)
He who knows my name.
He who kisses my hands
and tells me they are tools
for beauty, to be done
on this earth (Amen)
as it is in heaven.

"Just above my head
I hear singing in the air."
Reachable. In the span
of angels wings twisting
and breaking against the wind.
Within a maze of clouds
I see a haggard-face woman.

Oh, she is familiar.
She is tired.
She is strong.

Her flip-flops beat back
lightening and thunder
bolting beyond reach
hidden in blues blocking out
the mouth of a fire-spitting dragon.

She glides by as star after star
is felled by scaly tails of red.
I fear this face, this monstrous face.

I know I've seen it too before
when I was spirit not yet born.
Clustered beneath coils floating
in a water sac. I tell you,
there is some known thing
about this nameless creature

whose head arches above
the seventh heaven and tails
that blocks the thrones of sainted souls
who sit pondering. "What to do?"

A stone is thrown and pierces his hide.
From deep within a sound cries out.
"Lord my God! Have mercy on me."
And then I come forward trembling,
shouting. Crying out against a
tortuous fire burning the inside
of my mouth. It boils in a sea
of swill and bile in my stomach.
"Oh Lord, my God! Have mercy on me!"

Ritual

The ring of the sea as it sings in the evening
seeks to settle my soul in quiet dusk.
If salt stings my athlete feet, let it.
Serves me right, walking on briny grains.

Ah, but in sounds of Mahgrib prayers
my spirit basks in celestial promises.
Here the hounds of Harrow cannot
hear me when I sigh.

Let the wind song peel layers
of my eardrums so that the bells
of St. Michel's are dimmed.
Come, beat the drum, flagellate
so that ghosts of Chartres
cannot trace my fleeting feet.
Yes beat, beat the drum.
I am come! I am come!

Dance the dance that protects
our eyes against nutcrackers
of glaciered Steppes.
I am come! I am come! Ayi!
Ayi! Ayi!

Oh Earth of mine
dirt-dark like me,
I am come. I am come.
Seed of your womb,
branch of your tree,
I am come! I am come!

Is there grit of sand
bite of song that steals
more sweetly secrets
of an ebony night
than you, than you?

Again the wind howls.
Once more you come.
A ghost riding on a breeze.
Come to steal my heart
and remind me of my ties
to you, to you.

I approach and smells of pineapples
ripple in the air. Child, away, away.
Your skin is death-withered memories
of fried doh-doh and bonga.
When I reach to touch my hand
to your hand, press my heart
to yours, I see holes open.
Time-frozen cries of the ravished,
raise puckered pores of my skin.

Ah, will you not be still?
Can I not know one moment free
from you and ancestral thoughts?
Oh spirits, I am here. I am here!

Stars don't shine. The moon
an envious Market-Mami,
hordes ebah and kenkey
in pots of gold painted black
to shoo away birds and punish
fat city dwellers.

Had you been there stars,
you, like maidenhair
plaited and shy, dancing
beneath a night sky,
we could have found them,
the lost ones.

Beat the drum! Ayi, beat the drum!
We saw them run, heard their cries
that night, that night be damned.
No, no, no!

Are we not the darkest?
And in their haste
might not the gods punish us?
Are we not the darkest?
And in the night, holy night
where mystery uncovers
secrets of the day lay bare,
how do our souls fare?

Their hands may touch us
down there. And we will be
a tree cut down,
a race un-run,
cut off. Go!
Go I say!
What more do you want?
Have I not given you feet?

You have mastered neither
beat nor dance. You cannot
perform rites of purity.
Mixed! Hybrid!
Tree with no trunk.
Flowers dropping.
Now there is nothing
to remind us
of the old ways.
Ayi, The Ancestors stir!
They say, they say,
this is not the way
for man to do.

Ayi, their blood boils.
Rage displaces love
in a lover's eyes
before consummation.
Eya! where to go?
Which path to take?

To the South!
Leave no mine upstanding
no house un-felled.
I have given you feet.
What more do you want?

To the North!
Leave no hill untouched
nor sand dune piled high.
Turn grit to glass.
Don't let time pass
and slip away from us.

To the North!
Hide behind
the doors of the Kaybile.
This is your gift.
We your mothers
fathers, grandparents all
have given to you, my one.

Do not leave a gold weight,
or silken threads of Ananse.
Deny words to a brass bed
speaking in a larcenous tongue.
Spit out the cleansing water
less a despised Judas will
rain down the spoils of ruination.

West! West! Do not leave the old ways
for new too soon, lest you forget
times before you learn the truth.
Eh! What is it? This gold that runs
and blackens your hands?
You cannot cook until you've washed.

To the East! Do not desert the dawn
to hold up the sun alone. Nor hide
at noon reaching for a shadow
with whom to play touch and go.

Have I not given you feet?
This earth will decay.
Am I not of clay?
The seas churn
wash away seeds
implanted in goobah hills.
I say, are we not drum beats,
children of the moon?

This blood coursing through
the marrow of our being,
in rivers of spirits whose names
we no longer know, no longer call.

Remember, dried calabashes
are noisier. Have I not given
you feet? Must you have shoes?

Walk Together Children

In wind-swept rain drenched roads
imprints of tired feet, toilers of soil
indent men under sun-hot-hand;
tread on my rich red clay.

Into dust filled day air I scream
sorrowing-earth-mother-screams.
I watch my moonchildren's dreams
wash away on pirogues, on fish boats
and steamboats. I pray, "Lord, Lord,
watch over them." in dusty country air.

Walk together children! Don't get weary.
Come, place your head upon my breasts.
And we, Ibrahim and Haggar, will cradle you
under star-filled skies. Under night skies
where desert winds will softly cool you.
With my own hands I will wash
your travel-weary feet and sing.
"Dis one nah be mah pickin-o" song.

Walk on soft feet, fleet feet on gray
cold streets where green is absent.
Dirt clouds hang low. As low
as your brow. Your sad eyes
shield unshed loveless tears
for all the thing that might have been.
For lips that never cried from joy
nor love in tender words.
And in muted silence greet
your tramping sidewalk aching soles.

Come dear ones. and come closer still.
Let my ghost-ridden spirit bring you
a continent of deep dark dirt ever close
to your snow-chilled souls. Oh come,
come children. There's a big pot
boiling in my red kitchen.
The fire is hot.

Smell the fresh bread.
Let the wind whisper gently
around your head.
Let the steam rise slowly.
And let your mouth water.
Your head hang low.
So as to catch the smell.
So as to feel the warmth.
Let pepper sting your throat.
With my hand on your head
I shall wipe the water from your eyes.
Sing your earth love lullabies
and bless your soul above.

Bridges

"My soul looks back
and wonders, how I got over."

Hers was a hand of unexpected gifts
touching torn cuticles and finger-bitten quicks
She moved her eyes over me.
And walked her legs over shards of glass,
discarded garbage no one wants anymore.

Through this she came and went
taking me to another country
where I had the power to people it
with my hands and tongue.

I came crying and he held me close.
For the first time his hand was open.
They touched me minus the strap.

He could not speak, nor could I.
We were one within the four walls
in a rented storefront temple.

"Come ye disconsolate."
Sainted voices gave rise to song.
Sang words into my soul
and my heart rejoiced.

He sighed and unpinned his eyes
staring ahead. His breath boiled
in his barrel chest, raging against
approaching death.

He died. I looked down
with dried tears. A heavy hear
ladened with words years
had piled up but never passed my lips.
On top the sea and on a ship

sailing the same seas as them,
my grandfathers had come
so many years ago.

I am fearful. Where are they?
My eyes have searched
for familiar faces.
On seas I sail on the backs
of all the men; grandfathers,
uncles and unknowns
on a sea they sailed eons ago.

Surely there must be a heaven.
Earth has little place for peace.
The fifteen feet of air spacing
me from entrapped dwellers

of fourth-class cabins are the same
as sweat rife boats that carried
my fathers and their fathers, fathers
so very long ago.

This deja vu forms a cold ball
around by heart and fog
encircles my head.
A ghostly figure rises from the mist.
It follows me draped in a black coat.

He is unknown. I do not know his name.
Yet, I hear the wind whispering secrets.
No one taught me these sounds.
I can only speak the feel of spray.

But when I look down on the sea
I see drooped shoulders of men,
black breasts cupped in white hands,
silver chains sparkling in moonlight.

As I dream of evenings in Paris,
love under the Seine, Congo Square,
will not be erased from my mind.

I vomit up my hate.
Emptying myself into the sea
that carried my father.
I call his name. "Daddy."

Daddy, I am alone in the middle
of a dark and rolling ocean.
"I cannot swim. I cannot swim."

The black-draped figure
comes over to me,
extends its arms then,
I fly away to glory.

"Father, I stretch my hand to Thee."

Paris

Cobble stoned and cold
streets with rats and cats
whose languages I hear
but cannot comprehend.
Yet here I am in cafes
coffee by day, wine nightly.

My note pads fill with exes
and slashes. My room is not
Grandmother Saturdays.
It never smells clean.
But, something is here.

In smoked-filled clubs
up steep stairs I sit.
An artist in yellow
with dark brown hands
smiles kindly on me.

He tells me I am lovely.
My ears are even shaped.
My lips sensuous, full.
He is lover/brother
father/friend/god.

Molded am I of clay
and yielding sinews.
The river knows no parents.
Fine, I know no father.

Oh Paris, I have come
so far with so little.
No books to throw away.
No money to buy sheets.

Each day my pad grows.
My name sounds strange
on new lips and in new words.
Granny called me, "Sonny."
Here I am, "Gem-me."

Return

So now I am back.
I have come with
luggage and stories,
pictures and news clippings.

Back to this place,
a house my first book bought,
In the time spent away
how little has in fact changed.

Much is different and yes,
I have put on ten pounds.
It's all right you know.

We sit in the kitchen
face to face with eyes
searching for signs
of old habits and scars.

We both are getting older.
You had a head start.
Both our heads have beaten
against the walls of worlds

that tried to box us inside.
You show me each letter,
card I ever wrote. Trivia
at this moment is touching.

Behind the door snickering
and 'shhes,' smothered words
where second and third generations
wait to see 'Frog Eyes.'

Now when the door is open
silence and wonderment
greets my wildly beating heart.
There are no words of scorn
on their lips, nor in their eyes.

Oh God! They love me.
I am loved! I am loved!

La Neige

Cold and hard under our feet,
slipping and laughing, we braved
small roads of an obscure village
in the midst of snowy hills.

Our caps and coats speckled
with white flakes fall to the door
and track the floor of a cabin
we shelter and love.

Here we hid amongst those
whose only image of black
was ugly, sinful and fear
except when religious love
caused them to don costumes
and soot to buy a space in heaven.

Villagers dig inside their coffers
to send the holy word abroad
to the darkest regions of hell,
Africa, a place far beyond
snow capped mountains.

I say nothing of the gospel
burning in my heart. Rather,
I turn myself over to him.
When I see his body male
as mine, I am relieved
of the horrors of my ugliness.
In loving him I love me.

"Even my Lord, even me..."

Yes, I can love even this child/me
with no name of my own.
Whose first language was;
Cat, Dog, Rat and Roach.
Who now knows how to say,
"Mon cher, j'taime." and more.

What keeps my soul warmed
inside my cold body is not
a glazing fire nor soup
and cognac. It is a love
I only dreamed.

And when Bessie's
raucous voice
scares away
the cold god.
She melts
his iced fingers
threatening my fragile heart.

The End

Some have kept a vigil
as if to scare death
to keep him at bay.
But in the corner
of this house,
a masque of wood
is hung.

It smiles warm, friendly.
Opens its mouth to sing
of love beyond this room,
this bed, this earth.

If only I would come dance with him.
"Father, I stretch my hands to Thee."

It is a game of hide-and-seek
which the living play with death.
Each dances amongst shadows
seeking stars to brighten
the path to heaven.
Listen! Listen!
Someone is calling my name.
My name! How shall I call you?
Kini nshe nko?

So long and lost am I.
Seeking a safe haven.
Ah Lu——, no!
It is a name
I will whisper
only when
I am through with life.
Love is an epitaph
my heart echoes in the night.
Finally, all I want
is to be an honest man.
To write the sound
of Saturday and Sunday.

To accuse the tired week
of wasted workers, black
and sometimes sad.
Who know how to dance
and sing, cook and build.

When Bessie sings
her rambunctious soul
quiets at the throne of love.
And so, we go on and on,
dancing, singing, living, dying.

"Precious Lord, take my hand.
Lead me onnnnnn."